The Galapagos

Izabella Hearn

Level 1

Series Editors: Andy Hopkins and Jocelyn Potter

1.1 What's the book about?

What can you see in the picture? Do you know any of the names in your language? Which of them can you see in your country?

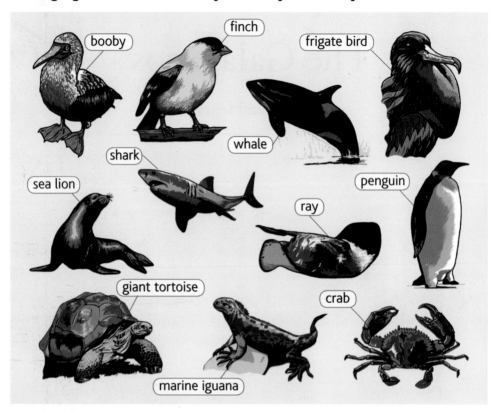

booby
finch
frigate bird
whale
shark
sea lion
ray
penguin
giant tortoise
crab
marine iguana

1.2 What happens first?

Look at the words at the bottom of pages 1–3. What are they in your language? Then look at the pictures on the same pages. Circle the right words in the sentences.

1 The Galapagos are in the *Atlantic / Pacific* Ocean.

2 Sophie and David are *working / on vacation* in the Galapagos.

3 They swim with *sharks / crabs*.

4 They see *sea lions / rays* under the water, too.

5 There is a very famous *giant tortoise / marine iguana* in the Galapagos.

The Amazing Galapagos 1

Sharks!

Sophie and David are making a movie for a famous American movie **festival**. It is about the Galapagos **Islands**. Today they are swimming with sharks.

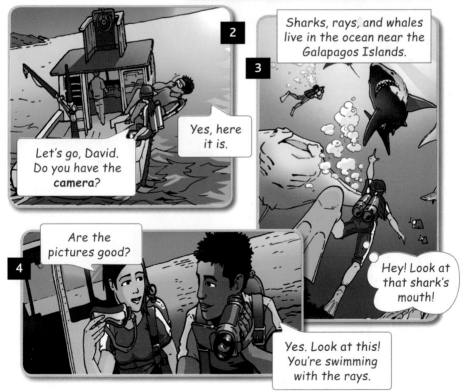

Sharks, rays, and whales live in the ocean near the Galapagos Islands.

Let's go, David. Do you have the **camera**?

Yes, here it is.

Are the pictures good?

Hey! Look at that shark's mouth!

Yes. Look at this! You're swimming with the rays.

festival /ˈfɛstəvəl/ (n) There is a *festival* here every year. People can watch interesting new movies.
island /ˈaɪlənd/ (n) I am going to swim to one of the *islands*.
camera /ˈkæmrə, -ərə/ (n) He is taking photos of his friends with his new *camera*.

1

The Galapagos Islands

The Galapagos Islands are **volcanoes**. They are in the Pacific Ocean. Some islands are very, very small and have no name. Some are big and people live on them.

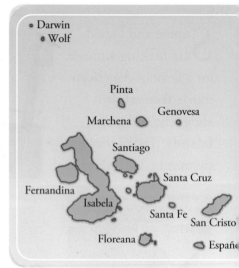

Visitors come to the islands by boat or by airplane. Many of them stay in the town of Puerto Ayora, on the island of Santa Cruz. There is a small town on San Cristobal, and a very small town, Villamil, on the island of Isabela. Isabela is a big island and has six volcanoes. This is sometimes a problem because animals and **birds** live near the volcanoes.

The islands are beautiful, but there is not much food and not much water. That is difficult for the animals, too. Only very strong animals can **survive**.

The Galapagos Islands are the home of the famous Galapagos giant tortoises. The giant tortoises can live with very little water and food, but they can't swim. They are very very big!

volcano /vɑlˈkeɪnoʊ/ (n) The animals are running away because noises are coming from the *volcano*.
bird /bɚd/ (n) There are a lot of *birds* in those trees.
survive /sɚˈvaɪv/ (v) They *survived* for weeks in the Himalayas with no food.

Lonesome George

Galapagos Islands

South America

Lonesome George lives in the Charles Darwin **Research Station**. Charles Darwin was a famous visitor to the islands in 1835, but now George is famous, too. He is the **last** giant tortoise from Pinta Island. He is very old. Maybe he is 100 years old—we don't know. George is big and strong. He is heavy, too, and he moves very slowly. He sleeps under a tree.

George likes eating green **plants**. On hot days he often sits quietly near the water. Sophie loves watching him.

A lot of people visit him. They take photos and write books about him. They make movies about him, too.

lonesome /ˈloʊnsəm/ (adj) There was only one, *lonesome* man on the boat.
research station /ˈrisətʃ ˌsteɪʃən, rɪˈsətʃ/ (n) What fruit is this? Let's ask people at the *research station*.
last /læst/ (adj) We have no water. That was the *last* bottle.
plant /plænt/ (n) There are beautiful green *plants* near the water.

Yesterday we were on the boat early in the morning. There were rays and sharks in the water. We swim with the sharks every day. I love it, but sometimes it's **dangerous**.

We have a lot of pictures for the movie. These sharks are **amazing**. Look at their eyes! They aren't friendly, but they're very interesting!

We arrived at our rooms near Puerto Ayora very late and it was dark. It's always dark at about 7 o'clock on the islands.

Suddenly, there was a light. It came from the island of Isabela. It was a volcano! We went quickly into the street.

There were a lot of people in the street and a lot of noise, too. Our friends from the hotel were there. They have a big boat. We went to Isabela with them and their friends.

Here's one of David's pictures of the volcano. Isn't it amazing?

dangerous /ˈdeɪndʒərəs/ (adj) The ocean is *dangerous* at night for small boats.
amazing /əˈmeɪzɪŋ/ (adj) He is very young, but he dances very well. He is *amazing*!

It was quiet on the island. There were noises from the volcano, but there were no birds or animals. We walked and walked to a small open place. There were no plants and no trees, but there was a giant tortoise. It didn't move, but it looked at us with small, unhappy eyes.

"How can animals survive the volcano? What can we do for them? How can we **help**?" we asked.

Our friends called the research station and a boat arrived with some **scientists**. The tortoise was big and heavy, and it didn't want to go. It was difficult, but the scientists moved it to the boat. David and I helped them and the tortoise went back to the research station. You can see it in this picture.

This tortoise is going to survive because the scientists are helping it. It's going to stay at the research station for some time. There it's going to have food and water and a home. Then it's going to go back to Isabela.

It's going to be OK, but was it the only tortoise near the volcano?

Tomorrow we're going to go to Isabela again. Every tortoise is important and we want to help all of them.

---

help /hɛlp/ (v) The people on that boat are having problems. Let's *help*!
scientist /ˈsaɪəntɪst/ (n) What's that light in the ocean? Maybe the *scientists* know.

2.1 Were you right?

Look at your answers to Activity 1.2 on page ii. Then finish the sentences.

Hello, Tony!

¹........................ and I are in the Galapagos now. We're making

our ²........................ for the festival. Every day we swim with

³........................ and ⁴........................ . Sometimes we see whales,

too! There's a famous ⁵... here.

His name is Lonesome ⁶........................ . He's very big and very

⁷........................ .

Is it cold in Boston? It's very ⁸........................ here.

With love,

Sophie

2.2 What more did you learn?

Are these sentences right (✓) or wrong (✗)?

1   The Galapagos are islands in the Pacific Ocean.

2   They are volcanoes.

3   No people live on the islands.

4   There are no towns.

5   Charles Darwin visited the islands in 1835.

6   There are a lot of animals in the Galapagos Islands.

7   Lonesome George has a big family.

8   He likes eating fish.

9   Sophie and David are staying on the island of Santa Cruz.

10   They help a sea lion on Isabela.

2.3 Language in use

Read the sentence on the right. Then finish sentences 1–6 with these verbs, in the past tense.

> We **arrived** at our rooms near Puerto Ayora very late and it **was** dark.

| survive move be go arrive be |

1 There ....was.... a light on Isabela.

2 We .... to the island with our friends.

3 There .... no plants near the volcano.

4 A giant tortoise ....

5 A boat ...., with some scientists.

6 The scientists .... the tortoise to their boat.

Now match the sentences with these pictures.

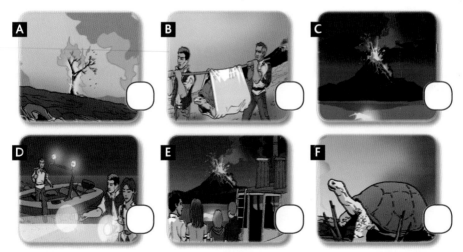

2.4 What happens next?

1 Talk about the pictures on pages 8–13. Which animals and birds can you see?

2 Look at the pictures on page 8 again. Where are David and Sophie going? Why? What is the problem on the boat?

The Amazing Galapagos 2

Watch that bird!

1 Sophie and David are going to go back to Isabela this morning.

2 David! It's late. Let's go by bike.

OK. Hey! Don't stand on the iguanas!

3 Look at those boobies! They're dancing!

Quick! The camera!

4 Oh, no! What's that? Hey! Stop!

5 Oh, David, that was my food!

Hey! Smile! You can have some of mine.

Hello from Sophie!

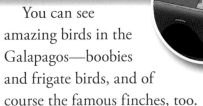

You can see amazing birds in the Galapagos—boobies and frigate birds, and of course the famous finches, too.

Some boobies have red **beaks**; some have blue feet. Their eyes are yellow and they can see very well. They live near the ocean and catch **fish**. They catch the fish under water.

Frigate birds live near the ocean, too, but they don't swim. They can't walk and many of them are very big and heavy. Frigate birds don't like catching fish. They don't like putting their beaks under water. They often take food from the birds on the islands.

beak /biːk/ (n) They take fruit from the trees with their long *beaks*.
fish /fɪʃ/ (n) The *fish* are swimming under our boat!

On the Beach

There is a lot of noise on the **beach** on the island of San Cristobal. It isn't the children from the town. It is the sea lions. In the day it is very hot and the young sea lions like playing in the water. Their mothers and fathers watch them. Then they come out of the water and sit on the beach. Sometimes they come onto the street and sit near a house or a store. Sometimes they sit on the beach chairs and watch people.

Sea lions have very good eyes. They can see the fish in the water. They like catching them. They like eating them, too. Sea lions are very heavy. They can't walk very quickly, but in the water they are amazing.

The water is often cold in the ocean near the Galapagos Islands, but the marine iguanas like it. They swim every day. They eat plants from the ocean. Then they come up and sit in the sun. They don't move very much and they are usually quiet. On the island of Fernandina marine iguanas are green and red, but usually they are black. They have small dark eyes and angry faces and they always sit near the water.

beach /bitʃ/ (n) Small children are playing on the *beach* near the boats.

There are penguins on the Galapagos Islands, too. Usually penguins live in very cold countries, but these are Galapagos penguins. They can survive in the Galapagos because the ocean is often cold. They stay near the water in the day. They love the water, but they don't like the long, hot days.

They are not very big, and they are not very tall. They usually have small families and they all eat fish.

You can see a lot of beautiful crabs in the Galapagos. Some are an amazing red color. Very young crabs are black. Some crabs are brown and have blue eyes. They have ten legs. They are not dangerous to people, but they eat … crabs!

We're working all day on the movie today. In the morning we went back to Isabela. The island was very quiet after the volcano, but it wasn't quiet at the research station!

Some scientists are looking at our tortoise and asking questions. How did it survive? Where did it come from? Is it a tortoise from Pinta Island? That was Lonesome George's home.

Maybe George has a family! Maybe he isn't the last! We don't know the answers, but the questions are very interesting.

There are a lot of tortoises at the research station. Some are only days old. Some are four or five months old. The scientists and students watch them. The big tortoises go back to their islands. The scientists take Española tortoises back to Española; Isabela tortoises go back to Isabela.

Charles Darwin

Sophie and David are not the first visitors to the Galapagos Islands. In 1835 Charles Darwin, a young man from England, came to the islands on his boat, the *Beagle*.

There were many interesting birds on the islands. They were small finches, but they were **different** on every island. Darwin watched the finches and started to ask questions.

"Why are the finches different?" he asked.

Their beaks were different because their food was different. Darwin started to understand. A long time before that, the finches were all the same. There were plants and **insects** on the islands. The finches wanted food. They wanted to survive. They wanted to eat the plants and the insects. Slowly their beaks **changed**. Now they can eat the different food on the different islands. Now the finches can survive.

Some years it is very hot. There is only a little water and the food changes. Maybe the finches' beaks are going to change again, too. The scientists in the Galapagos Islands are watching them.

There are thirteen families of finches on the islands. They are friendly birds and you can see them in the trees, on the beach, and in the towns.

Charles Darwin visited Ecuador, Argentina, and Chile. He visited Cape Town in South Africa and places in Australia. In every new place he looked at the plants and watched the animals and the birds. How did they survive? What made them strong? Darwin's book, *The Origin of Species*, is very famous and important. Scientists and students read it and talk about his work today, many years later.

different /ˈdɪfrənt/ (adj) This bike is *different*—mine is red.
insect /ˈɪnsɛkt/ (n) Small *insects* live in the fruit.
change /tʃeɪndʒ/ (v) His eyes were blue, but then they *changed*. Now they are brown.

3.1 Were you right?

Remember your answers to Activity 2.4. Then talk about this picture from Sophie and David's story. Answer these questions.

1 What can you see in the picture?

2 What did Sophie and David do before this?

3 What are they doing now?

4 What are they going to do?

3.2 What more did you learn?

Write *can* or *can't* in these sentences.

1 Boobies .... see very well.

2 They .... catch fish under water.

3 Frigate birds .... take food from birds' beaks.

4 Sea lions .... swim very well.

5 They .... walk quickly.

6 Marine iguanas .... swim.

7 Penguins .... survive in cold water.

8 They .... stay away from water in hot sun.

9 Crabs .... eat crabs.

10 Scientists .... watch a lot of Pinta Island tortoises.

11 Visitors .... see finches in towns.

12 We .... read Darwin's words today.

.3 Language in use

**Read the sentences on the right.
Then finish sentences 1–6
with these words.**

> Don't stand **on** the iguanas!
>
> Look **at** those boobies!

| in on about of to from |

1 Sophie and David went .... Isabela again.

2 There were a lot .... tortoises at the research station.

3 Lonesome George comes .... Pinta Island.

4 Charles Darwin asked questions .... finches.

5 There were a lot of different finches .... the islands.

6 Darwin watched animals and birds .... many different places.

.4 What happens next?

**Look at the pictures and answer the questions. Which is the
right answer (✓)?**

1 (page 16) What do
Sophie and David
help?

2 (page 17) They
make a new friend.
What is it?

3 (page 19) Where
are Sophie and
David?

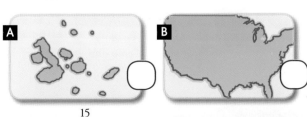

The Amazing Galapagos 3

Help!

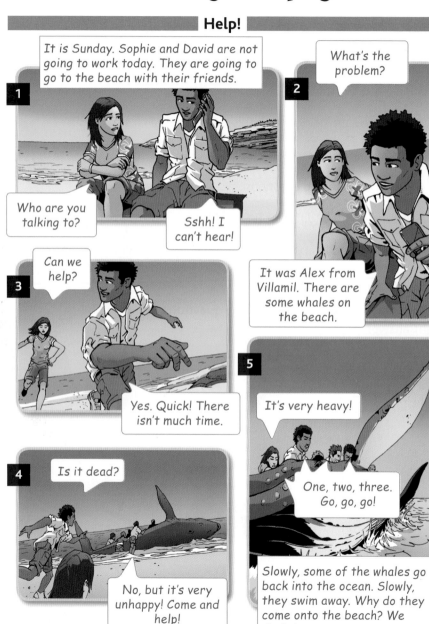

1 It is Sunday. Sophie and David are not going to work today. They are going to go to the beach with their friends.

Who are you talking to?

Sshh! I can't hear!

2 What's the problem?

3 Can we help?

It was Alex from Villamil. There are some whales on the beach.

Yes. Quick! There isn't much time.

5 It's very heavy!

One, two, three. Go, go, go!

4 Is it dead?

No, but it's very unhappy! Come and help!

Slowly, some of the whales go back into the ocean. Slowly, they swim away. Why do they come onto the beach? We don't know.

Hello from Sophie!

Today we're finishing the movie for the festival. It's beautiful and we're very happy with it. We have pictures of animals, birds, and plants. We have pictures of the volcano, the sharks, and the whales—and, of course, Lonesome George!

The tortoise on Isabela wasn't from his family, but the scientists are always looking for a Pinta Island tortoise. Sorry, George! Maybe one day …

We have a lot of friends here now. Here is our new friend, a whale shark! She wanted to swim with us all day. She waited for us in the afternoon and played with us again. Whale sharks are very big, but they're not dangerous. They don't swim very quickly and they don't eat people.

The islands are amazing and we don't want to go. We want to stay here!

The Amazing Galapagos 4

The new movie

Hey! Look, David! That's about our movie!

The New Galapagos Movie!

Where? The Beach Hotel
When? Saturday, March 26
What time? 6 o'clock

Please come—and bring your friends, too!

Come and see the new Galapagos movie. On Monday it is going to California, to the movie festival, but on Saturday you can see it here in Puerto Ayora!

We all know David and Sophie. We see them every day with their cameras and their smiles. This is their movie and it is amazing.

You can see whales, sharks, and rays in our oceans. There are penguins and iguanas on the beaches. Sea lions play with their young families. Boobies catch fish in the ocean.

Watch Sophie and David with the tortoises on Isabela. See their pictures of Lonesome George, and listen to the story of Charles Darwin and his famous book.

Why was Darwin's visit important? Why are our finches interesting?

Did the whales survive? Can we help the animals of the Galapagos?

Buy your tickets at the beach store. It is open every morning from 10 o'clock.

The movie festival

… and which movie did we like? The answer is … **The Amazing Galapagos** by Sophie and David. Come up here with us, please!

1

2

Sophie and David, here is $10,000 for you! Let's have a photo!

Thank you, thank you.

3

Talk to us about the islands, Sophie.

It wasn't a vacation—we worked every day and some nights, too.

But we loved it.

4

We don't know. Maybe …

What are you going to do with the money?

Yes, we do! We are going to go back to the Galapagos. We want to help the animals.

Talk about it

1 **Work with a friend.**

a | Student A | You are David's mother. You are talking to David on the telephone. Ask questions. Is he well? Does he like the Galapagos Islands? What did he do yesterday? What did he see? What is he going to do?

| Student B | You are David, and you are in the Galapagos Islands. Which day is it? Think about that. Then answer your mother's questions.

b | Student A | You are Sophie's father. You are talking to Sophie on the telephone. Ask questions about her time in California.

| Student B | You are Sophie. You are in California. It is the morning after the movie festival. Answer your father's questions.

2 **Work with two or three friends. Play this game.**

| Student A | Think of a Galapagos bird or animal. Answer your friends' questions. You can only give short answers with *Yes* or *No*.

| Students B–D | Which bird or animal is your friend thinking of? You can ask five questions.

Does it have blue feet?

No, it doesn't.

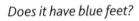

Write about it

1 **Write about an animal from the Galapagos.**

....

....

2 **Write about a bird.**

....

....

20

Scientists in every country watch animals and birds. How many different animals and birds are there? Why are they interesting? Work with a friend. You are going to watch birds.

1 **Talk about a time and a place.**

a At what time can you watch birds every day for a week? Early in the morning? Early in the evening?

b Where can you watch them? In your yard or a friend's yard? Is there a place with trees near your house?

2 **Find the names of birds in English.**

Which birds are you going to see? What do you think? Write four bird names in your language and then find their names in English. Look in a dictionary or on the Internet.

Your language	English
1	....
2	....
3	....
4	....

3 **Watch the birds.**

Write the names of the birds from Activity 2 here. Then start to watch the birds.

a Do you see those birds? On which days? Check (✓) them.

b Do you see different birds? Write their names and check (✓) them.

Name of bird	Mon	Tues	Wed	Thurs	Fri	Sat	Sun

4 Write a report about your Bird Watch. What was interesting?

Bird Watch Report

Names of students: ....
....
....
....

Place: ....

Time: ....

BIRDS

1 Name: ....   How many days? ....

2 Name: ....   How many days? ....

3 Name: ....   How many days? ....

4 Name: ....   How many days? ....

5 Name: ....   How many days? ....

6 Name: ....   How many days? ....

7 Name: ....   How many days? ....

Notes:
....
....
....
....
....

5 Talk about a bird.

a Choose one of your birds. Read about it in books or on the Internet. Where does it live? Does it stay in one place all year? What does it eat? Why is it interesting?

b Give a short talk about the bird. Then answer questions.